G000107881

OVALHOUSE

Paper Tiger and **Ovalhouse** present

SOUR LIPS
by Omar El-Khairy

First performed on 29 January 2013 at Ovalhouse

SOUR LIPS
by Omar El-Khairy

CAST

Tom MacMaster	**Simon Darwen**
Amina Arraf	**Lara Sawalha**
Chorus 1	**Celine Rosa Tan**
Chorus 2	**Takunda Kramer**
Chorus 3	**Eden Vik**

CREATIVE AND PRODUCTION TEAM

Playwright	**Omar El-Khairy**
Director	**Carissa Hope Lynch**
Producer	**Iain Goosey**
Designer	**Florence McHugh**
Lighting Designer	**Joshua Pharo**
Sound Designer	**Tom Wilson**
Associate Director	**Gary Horner**
Casting Director	**Gemma Lloyd**
Stage Manager	**Phillip Richardson**
Press	**Alice Baynham**
Trailer	**Dan Patrick Hipkin / TEAfilms Ltd**
Print design	**Matthew Wright**
Image	**Tanya Habjouqa**

Sour Lips was originally developed through the Ovalhouse FiRST BiTE programme in May 2012, before being commissioned as a co-production with Paper Tiger to open Ovalhouse's Counterculture 50 Season.

This production is funded by Arts Council England via the National Lottery. The writing of this play was also assisted by a grant from The Peggy Ramsay Foundation.

Supported using public funding by
ARTS COUNCIL
LOTTERY FUNDED **ENGLAND**

Paper Tiger would like to thank Steve Elder, Lisa Came, Amna Hafiz, Amy Riddell, Pablo Baz, Rachel Briscoe and all of the Ovalhouse team, fellow Paper Tigers Tanya Singh and Afsaneh Gray and Mr and Mrs El-Khairy for their translation skills.

CAST

Simon Darwen | Tom MacMaster
Theatre credits include *Mad About the Boy* (Young Vic / Bush Theatre / Unicorn / National Tour), Petruchio in *The Taming of the Shrew* (Southwark Playhouse), *Unrestless* by Ben Ellis (Old Vic Tunnels), *Accolade* (Finborough Theatre), *Love Love Love* by Mike Bartlett (Original Cast – Paines Plough / Drum Theatre Plymouth / National Tour), *Ramshackle Heart* (Public Theatre New York), *Shove, Arse* by Colin Teevan (Theatre503), *Mad Forest* by Caryl Churchill (BAC), *Johnny Macabe* (Arcola), *Signs of Rust* by Ben Ellis (Theatre503), *The Taming of the Shrew, The Merchant of Venice, A Midsummer Night's Dream* and *The Tragedy of Thomas Hobbes* by Adriano Shaplin (RSC), *Fanny and Faggot* by Jack Thorne (Trafalgar Studios), *1 in 5* by Penny Skinner (Hampstead Theatre), *The Wonder: A Woman Keeps a Secret* (BAC), *Romance* by Al Smith (Old Vic New Voices), *24 Hour Plays / Ready* by Joel Horwood (Old Vic), *Nikolina, Flamingos, The Taste of It, Capital* (Nabokov). Television credits include *The Bill*.
Film credits include *Morris: A Life With Bells On*.

Takunda Kramer | Chorus 2
Takunda studied at the Royal Academy of Dramatic Art. Theatre credits include *Midnight Train to Sunrise* (Tiata Fahodzi / Africa Centre), *Twelfth Night* (Orange Tree Theatre), *Visiting Hour* (Phoenix Players), *A Raisin in the Sun* (Phoenix Players), *Who's Who* (Phoenix Players). Theatre at RADA includes *Five Years On* and *School for Scandal* (RADA).

Lara Sawalha | Amina Arraf
Lara studied at the Italia Conti Academy of Theatre Arts in London. Theatre credits include various *Political Satire* plays in Amman, Jordan with Nabil Sawalha and the Nabil Sawalha comedy group. Further theatre credits include *Prophet in Exile* (Chelsea Theatre, London), *Breaking News: The Story of Rachel Corrie – Parallel* (Theatre503), *Memoirs of Solitude* (Royal Cultural Center in Amman, Jordan), *Petra Rocks* (Amman, Jordan), *Rest Upon the Wind* (Tristan Bates Theatre / Riverside Studios).
Film credits include *High Heels* (SAE), *The Last Friday* (Royal Film Commission), *Father is Doing Fine* (brave new work Filmproduktions).
Various radio commercials in Amman, Jordan, including hosting the 2-hour show *Lipstick Lunch* (Radio Energy 97.7 – Amman, Jordan).

Celine Rosa Tan | Chorus 1
Celine studied at the Royal Conservatoire of Scotland. Theatre credits include *Cabaret* (Toy Factory Theatre Ensemble, Singapore), *Godspell* (All Good Gifts, Singapore), *Blithe Spirit* (Wild Rice Theatre, Singapore), *The Full Monty* (Pangdemonium Theatre, Singapore), *Sunday in the Park with George* (C Venues, Edinburgh), *Show Choir* (C Venues, Edinburgh). Film credits include *Sing to the Dawn* (Raintree Pictures) and voiceover *Oh Sylvia* (Heavy Entertainment) directed by Dawn French.

Eden Vik | Chorus 3
Eden trained at the Guildford School of Acting in Musical Theatre. Theatre credits include *L for Latch-Key*, *Leading the Witness* (Upstairs at the Gatehouse), *Being Norwegian* (Karamel Club), *Ivanov* (Theatre Collection), *A Memory, A Monologue, A Rant and A Prayer* (The Bussey Building), *Women's Revenge* (Best Female Act Award, Theatre Collection Solo Festival 2011), *Joy Division* (Practical Productions) and *Lady Eros* (Humanitas Culture). As a singer Eden has performed with the West End Chorus in *Chess* (Royal Albert Hall). For the Venetian Macau (China) she performed at concerts and events in Hong Kong and Macau. In her hometown Oslo, Eden has performed in *Company* (Oslo Central Teater) and *Les Misérables in Concert* (Oslo Spektrum).

CREATIVE TEAM

Omar El-Khairy | Playwright
Omar El-Khairy is a writer for stage and screen. He is a graduate of both the Court and the Soho Young Writers' Programmes and a fellow of the Old Vic New Voices T. S. Eliot UK / US Exchange. He is co-founder of the international theatre and film collective Paper Tiger.

His first full-length play *Given the Times* was commissioned for a rehearsed reading at the Finborough Theatre as part of Vibrant – A Festival of Finborough Playwrights. His other work for theatre includes *Return to Sender* (Orange Tree Theatre), *Polling Booth* (Theatre503), *Eyelids* (Unicorn Theatre), *Lovestrong* (The Lyric Hammersmith), *Burst* (Zoo Venues, Edinburgh), *Longitude* (The Public Theater, NYC) and *The Ark* (Arcola Theatre).

For screen, his short *Tunnels* is in post-production with Idioms Film in the West Bank and he is now developing his first feature length screenplay, *Sheikh*.

He also holds a PhD in Political Sociology from the LSE.

Carissa Hope Lynch | Director
Carissa Hope Lynch is a director and dramaturg from Manila by way of San Francisco. She trained at the University of California and Central School of Speech and Drama and now holds the position of Senior Reader at the Royal Court. Theatre direction includes *Securing Your World* (Bush Theatre), *Echo* (Ovalhouse FiRST BiTE), *Cracking* (New Wimbledon Theatre Studio), *Shepperton Road* (Rosemary Branch), and *Rather Than Words Comes the Thought of High Windows* (Market Estate Project).

As a dramaturg, *Reasons to be Cheerful* (National Tour), *Prometheus Awakes* (Greenwich and Docklands International Festival), *The Garden* (London 2012 Festival), and *The Iron Man* (Brighton Festival, GDiF).

Carissa has delivered research papers at Theatre Applications and TaPRA. Her photographic essay *The Bal Basera Project* was published in RiDE, and she co-authored a book chapter with Jenny Sealey for *Identity, Performance and Technology*.

Iain Goosey | Producer

Iain studied Drama and Theatre at Royal Holloway, University of London. He is a founding member and Producer of Waking Exploits, now one of Wales' leading project funded touring companies – www.wakingexploits.co.uk. Producing credits for Waking Exploits include *Serious Money* by Caryl Churchill (Waking Exploits / Tour), *Pornography* by Simon Stephens (Waking Exploits / Tour) and *Love and Money* by Dennis Kelly (Waking Exploits / Tour), with original work premiering around the UK in 2013. Further lead producing credits include *Caligula* by David Greig (Chapter Arts Centre / August 012 Ltd), *Sour Lips* by Omar El-Khairy (Ovalhouse / Paper Tiger) and *Robin Hood* (The Albany / Rich Mix / Gameshow). Iain has also received training through the Stage One programme for producers from Andrew Treagus, Mark Rubinstein and Nick Salmon.

Florence McHugh | Designer

Florence trained on The Motley Theatre Design Course. Theatre credits include *Office 925* (Live Theatre Newcastle), *Beyond the Pale* (Southwark Playhouse), Roundabout (The Bush Theatre / Theatre Delicatessen), *The Forecast* (Greenwich Playhouse), *Never Enough to live in the Now* (Hampstead Theatre Downstairs), *Julius Caesar* (Shilpakola National Theatre of Bangladesh & National tour), *Invasion!* (Selkirk Tooting), *In Quest of Conscience* (Finborough Theatre), *Change* (Arcola Theatre), *Cracking* and *The Choir* (both New Wimbledon Theatre), *Hidden Glory* and *The Song of Deborah* (both The Lowry), *Waiting for Godot* (BeMe Theatre Munich).

Costume Design credits include *Instants* (The Linbury Studio Royal Opera House), *Love's Labours Lost* (Guildford Castle), and *100 Shining Hearts* (The Palace Theatre Southend).

For film, Production Designer for the feature *Animal* and the short film *Roadkiller*.

Joshua Pharo | Lighting Designer
Joshua trained at Rose Bruford College of Theatre & Performance and now works across theatre, dance, opera, music, film & art installation as both a lighting designer and projection designer.
Recent credits include *Trojan Women* and *The Prophet* (The Gate), *Kreutzer Sonata* (The Gate / La Mama NYC), *Revolutions in Costume* (V&A Museum / LCF), *The Raphael Room*, *Purge* (Borealis Theatre / Arcola), *Do We Look Like Refugees?* (National Theatre Studio), *The Infant* (Les Enfants Terribles).
Joshua also works with musicians, designing responsive live environments. Current artists include *Saint Saviour* (International Tour), *Ultraista* (International Tour).
www.joshuapharo.co.uk

Tom Wilson | Sound Designer
Tom studied on the Recording Arts programme at SAE Institute and now works as a sound recordist, producer and engineer for music, film, theatre and radio. His recent work includes *el Constructor* by Colin Hickey and *Notes on Becoming a Liar* by Adam Wilson Hunter. He is currently working as a radio studio engineer and consultant on a number of radio broadcasts, including *Field Day Radio*. Tom has also worked as sound technician at HighTide Festival, and part of the sound crew for Philip Glass' *Einstein on the Beach* and Complicite's *The Master and Margarita* at the Barbican.
www.tomwilsonsound.co.uk

Gary Horner | Associate Director

Gary trained as an actor at Guildford School of Acting and has worked throughout the UK in film, theatre, television and radio. He also holds a Masters Degree in Voice Studies from Central School of Speech and Drama. Directing credits include *Agamemnon*, *Euripides* and *Love and Madness* (Academy of Live and Recorded Arts), *Ship Ahoy* and *The Wild Rumpus* (Art Burst Ltd) and was also assistant director on the development of *Sour Lips* (Ovalhouse).

Voice coaching includes *Romeo and Juliet* (The Chocolate Factory), *Reverie* (The Pleasance Theatre, Edinburgh), *The Arsonists* (Watford Palace Theatre), *In His Image* (Hampstead Theatre), *The Scarlet Pimpernel* (The Tower of London) and the award-winning *Play on Words* (Tristan Bates Theatre). Gary currently teaches voice and text at Mountview, East 15 and ALRA drama schools in London.

Gemma Lloyd | Casting Director

Gemma is a casting director and producer for film and theatre and director of act up, an independent acting and communication skills training organisation – www.act-up.co.uk. She also promotes and manages the spoken word collective Chill Pill, 6 actors, a band, a singer and an MC. Casting for theatre includes Omar El-Khairy's *Sour Lips* (Ovalhouse), *Screwed* (Pleasance Theatre), *Venus/Mars* (Old Red Lion Theatre), *Happy Birthday Wanda June* (Old Red Lion Theatre), *Pop* (Tristan Bates Theatre), *Sam Rose in the Shadows* (RichMix/UK Tour), *One Flea Spare* (Old Red Lion Theatre).

Film includes *Calloused Hands* (Jesse Quinones), *Feud* (Courttia Newland), *Full* (In-Sook Chappell), *People Won't Understand* (Shekhar Bassi), *Triangles* (Graham Taylor), *Mercutio's Dreaming: The Killing of a Chinese Actor* (Daniel York).

Paper Tiger symbolises contradiction. *Paper* is culture, thought, social order. *Tiger* is force, instinct, the wild. A paper tiger is simultaneously delicate and immense, fragile and ferocious, beautiful and with a bite.

Paper Tiger are a collective of emerging theatre and film-makers, working collaboratively and autonomously to create innovative new work. The company have backgrounds in theatre, film, performance, literature, dance, art, design, education and participatory practice.

The company, made up of Omar El-Khairy, Tanya Singh, Carissa Hope Lynch and Afsaneh Gray, passionately believe that being inventive with form is not only about pushing the boundaries of style or media or technique, but also about questioning forms of authorship.

Paper Tiger's practice is informed by varied disciplinary backgrounds, and has involved: site-responsive promenade, new writing, physical theatre, multimedia, archival work and radical adaptations. The company's aesthetic, stories and roles are not codified or fixed, but instead responsive to ideas. Narrative and performance are at the core of every Paper Tiger project, whether it takes place on a stage, a screen, the street or the web.

For more information on Paper Tiger, visit
www.papertiger.org.uk

OVALHOUSE

Anti-heroes and underdogs.
Stories told sideways.
The things under the bed.
Theatre for people with something to say.
New work for new audiences.

Since the 1960s, Ovalhouse has been a pioneering supporter of queer, feminist and diverse performance work. We remain committed to challenging preconceptions of what theatre is and can be.

Ovalhouse's current programme embodies our commitment to true artistic diversity, our appetite for experimentation with form and our dedication to process.

ovalhouse.com | @ovalhouse | @ovaldirector

SPRING 2013 – COUNTERCULTURE 50

In 2013, Ovalhouse celebrates its 50th birthday. For some of that 50 years, fringe theatre stood as a defiant counterpoint to the prevalent culture; work that critiqued the mainstream, explored questions it was afraid to ask, offered an alternative cultural experience. Is that still true today or was the idea of counter-culture quietly decommissioned when no one was looking? And if it was, when will we start to miss it?

Counterculture 50 is part retrospectacle, part theatrical incubator of a more politically-engaged performance future. It acknowledges the shoulders of giants, heroes and villains on which Ovalhouse stands. It asks how, why and when counterculture is possible. It is urgently hopeful, stealthily meaningful and there will also be funny bits.

60s: *The Act* by Thomas Hescott | 29 Jan – 2 Feb

70s: *Crimplene Millionaire* by Boogaloo Stu | 5 – 9 Feb

80s: *The Lady's not for Walking Like An Egyptian*
by Mars.tarrab | 12 – 16 Feb

90s: *Love On Trial* by Bilimankhwe Arts | 19 -23 Feb

00s: *Kinky* by 2HeadedPigeon | 26 Feb – 2 March

Sour Lips by Omar El-Khairy | 29 Jan – 16 Feb 2013

Freakoid by Emma Adams | 19 Feb – 9 March 2013

Your Place or Mine? by Tim Redfern and David Sheppeard | 26 Feb – 2 March

The Forest and the Field by Chris Goode & Company | 6 – 8 March 2013

Ovalhouse | 52-54 Kennington Oval | London | SE11 5SW
Tel: 020 7582 0080 | Box Office: 020 7582 7680 | info@ovalhouse.com

Ovalhouse

Theatre
Directors of Theatre: **Rebecca Atkinson-Lord & Rachel Briscoe**
Producer: **Faith Dodkins**
Theatre Manager: **Aaron Lamont**
Technical Manager: **Pablo Fernandez-Baz**

Front of House
Box Office and Theatre Supervisor: **Alex Clarke**
Duty Managers: **Ros Bird, Amirah Garba, Emily Wallis**
Front of House Assistants: **Tex Vincent Bishop, Tracey Brown, Justin Chinyere, Lorren Comert, Eric Geynes, Soniya Kapur, Michael Salami, Sofia Stephanou, Bevan Vincent**

Marketing
Head of Press & Marketing: **Debbie Vannozzi**
Press & Marketing Assistant: **Amelia De-Felice**
Archivist: **Rabyah Manzoor**

Executive
Director: **Deborah Bestwick**
General Manager: **Wendy Dempsey**

Development
Head of Fundraising: **Martyn Holland**

Administration
Finance Manager: **Tony Ishiekwene**
Administrative Manager: **Annika Brown**

Participation
Director of Participation: **Stella Barnes**
Head of Youth Arts: **Toby Clarke**
Head of Arts Inclusion: **Emily Doherty**
Arts Education Assistant: **Halima Chitalya**
Creative Producer – Truth About Youth: **Ruth Hawkins**
Pastoral Care and Monitoring Officer: **Jeanie Reid**
Creative Youth Inclusion Co-ordinator: **Lara Stavrinou**

Board
Martin Humphries: Chair
Merle Campbell: Deputy Chair
Sola Afuape: Treasurer
Graham Wiffen: Company Secretary
Oladipo Agboluaje
Mike Bright
Esther Leeves
Layla McCay
John Spall
Brian Walters

This text went to press before the end of rehearsals
and so may differ slightly from the play as performed.

For my parents

And in loving memory of Capital STEEZ

Omar El-Khairy

SOUR LIPS

OBERON BOOKS
LONDON
WWW.OBERONBOOKS.COM

First published in 2013 by Oberon Books Ltd
521 Caledonian Road, London N7 9RH
Tel: +44 (0) 20 7607 3637 / Fax: +44 (0) 20 7607 3629
e-mail: info@oberonbooks.com
www.oberonbooks.com

Copyright © Omar El-Khairy, 2013

Omar El-Khairy is hereby identified as author of this play in
accordance with section 77 of the Copyright, Designs and Patents
Act 1988. The author has asserted his moral rights.

All rights whatsoever in this play are strictly reserved and
application for performance etc. should be made before
commencement of rehearsal to Curtis Brown Group Ltd.,
Haymarket House, 28-29 Haymarket, London, SW1Y 4SP
(cb@curtisbrown.co.uk). No performance may be given unless
a licence has been obtained, and no alterations may be made in
the title or the text of the play without the author's prior written
consent.

You may not copy, store, distribute, transmit, reproduce or
otherwise make available this publication (or any part of it) in
any form, or binding or by any means (print, electronic, digital,
optical, mechanical, photocopying, recording or otherwise),
without the prior written permission of the publisher. Any person
who does any unauthorized act in relation to this publication may
be liable to criminal prosecution and civil claims for damages.

A catalogue record for this book is available from the British Library.

PB ISBN: 978-1-84943-476-8
E ISBN: 978-1-84943-797-4

Cover design by Tanya Hajouqa

Printed, bound and converted
by CPI Group (UK) Ltd, Croydon, CR0 4YY.

Visit www.oberonbooks.com to read more about all our books
and to buy them. You will also find features, author interviews and
news of any author events, and you can sign up for e-newsletters
so that you're always first to hear about our new releases.

DISCLAIMER

This play is a fictional account, which has been inspired by both a hoax and its true story. It contains extracts from Tom MacMaster's weblog, *A Gay Girl in Damascus*. However, the characters, timelines and incidents have been changed for dramatic purposes. In some cases, fictitious characters and incidents have been further added to the narrative, and the words are those imagined by the author. The play should not be understood as either a biography or factual account.

It will always be impossible to know, for the good reason that all writing is itself this special voice, consisting of several indiscernible voices, and that literature is precisely the invention of this voice, to which we cannot assign a specific origin: literature is that neuter, that composite, that oblique into which every subject escapes, the trap where all identity is lost, beginning with the very identity of the body that writes.

– Roland Barthes

Exile, in the words of Wallace Stevens, is "a mind of winter" in which the pathos of summer and autumn as much as the potential of spring are nearby but unobtainable. Perhaps this is another way of saying that a life of exile moves according to a different calendar.

– Edward Said

Acknowledgments

Thanks to Ovalhouse artistic directors Rachel and Rebecca for their belief and wholehearted commitment to the play from its very inception. I owe a huge debt of gratitude to many people who have helped develop the play and realise this production. They know who they are, and I am humbled by their kindness and insight. Thanks to friends and mentors who have always encouraged my writing and believed that this day would eventually come. Much love to Professor Paul Gilroy for his patience and understanding when I should have been working on my thesis. To my secondary school English teachers – Mr. Venning and Mr. Sutcliffe – never in your wildest dreams did you ever see this coming.

And to my Paper Tiger crew – Carissa, Tanya and Bubbles – we're on one.

Author's Note

All direction for the Chorus should be discovered by the director and cast in rehearsal. The Chorus should be on stage at all times and thus serve the story – both through song and physical language, as well as by bringing fluidity to the transitions between time and space. The cast should seek to blur the lines between characters and choral personalities, so that the Chorus holds the play together by pulling it apart. Choral lines and verses can and should be performed in an array of languages, but this is at the director's discretion.

All underlined text should be spoken in different languages – Amina's must be in Arabic. At no point in the performance should surtitles be employed. The various languages should be trusted.

The Chorus represents the infotainment telesector, which comprises those who create and control the world of signs and symbols through which all information, communication and entertainment are mediated.

The performance should convey the pace, rhythm and feel of our online lives.

The director should use their artistic discretion to adhere to these instructions or not, based on having a clear alternative vision that will also best serve the performance.

Characters

in order of appearance

CHORUS
see author's note

TOM MACMASTER
forty-year-old American graduate student

AMINA ABDALLAH ARRAF AL OMARI
twenty-five-year-old Syrian American blogger and activist

A dash (–) denotes an interruption or change in thought/intention in dialogue.

A forward slash (/) denotes an interruption by another character so that lines might overlap.

An asterix (*) denotes whole lines spoken simultaneously.

An ellipses […] denotes a silent but distinct response.

Setting
Somewhere between Edinburgh and Damascus. February – June 2011

Sour Lips was first performed at Ovalhouse, as part of their FiRST BiTE Counter-Culture Season of works-in-progress, on 31 May 2012. It was performed by Steven Elder, Lisa Came and Amna Hafiz.

An almost bare room. Two black plastic chairs. A free-standing full-length mirror. Old television sets stacked in opposite corners. In another corner sits a record player. Three microphone stands on a raised platform. All props are laid out neatly on the floor in front of the chairs. The room feels outer-worldly, yet it still conveys a certain sense of familiarity.

An overwhelming chaotic soundscape made up of film clips, live music recordings, news reports, archival material, found sounds, recorded voices and whispers.

The CHORUS is stood on the raised platform.

PROLOGUE

Asmahan's 'Once I Entered a Garden' is playing.

TOM carries AMINA on stage.

TOM delicately places AMINA on the second plastic chair. He strokes her hair gently. Lifeless, she sits still and stares into the audience.

TOM: *(Whispering.)* I want to see inside you.

Let me in – beneath your beauty.

You can trust me.

(Pause.)

TOM begins setting up the stage.

(Long pause.)

TOM: There's nothing like war for the reinvention of lives.

She was persuasive. She reminded me how ugly and violent it would be. It was important that I knew, she whispered to me. That I understood how painful it would be – for everyone.

But I still believed that her beginning would be different. That she would create a different future for all of us – one not born in flames.

You see, the old world is beginning to crumble and a new one has already begun – like scorched earth.

THE MACHINE RUMBLES

TOM: Hear that?

AMINA: […]

TOM: Did you hear that?

   (Beat.) Who's there?

   (Silence.)

CHORUS 1: Her words shine new light on an ever-troubled region.

CHORUS 2: Hers is the voice of a new generation.

CHORUS 3: She has helped capture the imagination of the Syrian opposition.

   (Faster.)

CHORUS 1: Frank.

CHORUS 2: Witty.

CHORUS 3: Heart-wrenching.

   (Slower.)

CHORUS 1: She has helped awaken the youth from their slumber.

CHORUS 2: She broaches subjects long-considered taboo in Arab culture.

CHORUS 3: Her voice must not go unheard.

   (Faster.)

CHORUS 1: Insightful.

CHORUS 2: Engaging.

CHORUS 3: Brutally honest.

   (Slower.)

CHORUS 1: What a time to be an Arab!

CHORUS 2: What a time to be in the Middle East!

CHORUS 3: What a time to be alive!

   The sound of barking.

(Silence.)

More intense barking.

(Silence.)

AMINA'S ABDUCTION

TOM: 2011.

    Monday. June 6th.

AMINA: Six p.m.

TOM: Abbasid bus station.

AMINA: Near Fares al Khouri Street.

    AMINA picks up a mobile phone.

TOM: Menu. Write. Message.

    AMINA starts texting.

    (Pause.)

TOM: Send.

    (Pause.)

TOM: Traffic.

    The sound of rush hour traffic.

    (Pause.)

TOM: Horns.

    The sound of car horns bellowing out.

    (Pause.)

TOM: Life.

CHORUS 1: <u>God is the greatest.</u>

    <u>God is the greatest.</u>
    <u>God is the greatest.</u>
    <u>God is the greatest.</u>
    <u>I bear witness that there is no deity except God.</u>
    <u>I bear witness that there is no deity except God.</u>
    <u>I bear witness that Muhammad is the Messenger of God.</u>

I bear witness that Muhammad is the Messenger of God.
Come to prayer.
Come to prayer.
Come to success.
Come to success.
God is greater.
God is greater.
There is no deity except God.

(Pause.)

CHORUS 2: Taxi. Taxi.
Al-Marjeh. Thank you.

CHORUS 3: Malboro, Cleopatra, Davidoff, Al Sherek, Benson & Hedges, Viceroy.

CHORUS 1: *(Lighting a cigarette.)* Two sandwiches. Falafel. More tahina. *(Beat.)* More. *(Beat.)* That's enough.

(Pause.)

CHORUS 1: And a Cola. *(Beat.)* Make it a 7 Up.

CHORUS 3: Please. Some change. Anything. *(Beat.)* Chewing gum. Fifty piastres.
Come on. Just fifty.
What is it to you?

CHORUS 1: Come on. Hey. *(Beat.)* No. Your friend.
Don't be shy girl. Your eyes – they're like flawless diamonds.
Come on. Give me your number. I won't bite. I promise.

(Pause.)

CHORUS 1: Pull over.
Driver's license.
Do you know this man?

(Beat.) Where you going?

CHORUS 2: Al-Marjeh.

CHORUS 1: I.D.

CHORUS 2 hands over his I.D.

CHORUS 1: *(Beat.)* <u>Get out of the car.</u>

    (Pause.)

TOM: No reception.

    Message pending.

AMINA: She said she'd be here. She said at this corner.

    I shouldn't have /

TOM: / <u>Peace be upon you.</u>

AMINA: *(Beat.)* <u>May peace be upon you.</u>

TOM: Are you waiting for someone?

AMINA: No.

TOM: From the Local Coordinating Committee?

AMINA: […]

TOM: Salma. *(Beat.)* Is that who you're waiting for?

AMINA: […]

TOM: Don't be afraid. You can answer me.

AMINA: Who are you?

    What do you /

TOM: / Don't worry. *(Offering his hand.)* I'm a friend of hers.

    AMINA is abducted.

    (Pause.)

TOM: Amina Arraf, a prominent Syrian American blogger, was kidnapped in Damascus yesterday by several unidentified men. Accompanied by a friend, she had gone to meet someone involved with the Local Coordinating Committee. She told her friend that she would go ahead and they were quickly separated. Amina had apparently identified the person she was to meet. However, while her companion was still close by, Amina was seized by three men in their early twenties.

According to one eyewitness – who does not want her identity to be known – the men were armed. Amina hit one of them and told her friend to go find her father. One of the men then put his hand over Amina's mouth and bustled her into a red Dacia Logan with a window sticker of Basel Assad. The witness did not manage to make out the number plate. The men are assumed to be members of the Ba'ath Party militia or one of the other security services. Amina's present location is unknown and it is still unclear whether she is in a jail or being held elsewhere in Damascus.

TOM creates his muse.

AMINA: *(Staring at TOM.)* <u>Alif. Ba. Ta. Tha. Gim. Ha.</u>

(Pause.)

AMINA: My name.

TOM: *(Looking at AMINA.)* […]

AMINA: My name.

(Pause.)

TOM: Her name.

AMINA: My name is.

TOM: Wait. Slow down.

AMINA: […]

TOM: Her name –

AMINA: *(Looking at TOM.)* […]

TOM: No. Let me –

Her name will be –

(Pause.)

TOM: *(Pointing to a headscarf.)* Put it on.

AMINA: […]

TOM: Go on.

AMINA takes the headscarf and puts it on.

(Pause.)

TOM: *(Looking at AMINA.)* Perfect.

    (Pause.)

TOM: And her name will be – Amina.

AMINA: […]

    (Pause.)

TOM: Say it.

    My name is.

AMINA: I don't /

TOM: / Say it.

    (Pause.)

AMINA: <u>My name is Amina.</u>

TOM: No. *(Beat.)* In English.

AMINA: *(Beat.)* My name is Amina.

TOM: Again.

AMINA: My name is Amina.

TOM: Again.

AMINA: My name is Amina.

TOM: Again.

AMINA: My name is Amina.

    (Pause.)

TOM: Good.

AMINA: […]

TOM: Now. *(Beat.)* Tell them.

    (Pause.)

AMINA: […]

TOM: Go on.

    Speak.

    (Pause.)

TOM: February 19th 2011.

AMINA: I was born in Aleppo.

My /

TOM: / No. That's not right.

Start again.

(Beat.) I was born in Staunton Virginia. To Abdallah Ismail Arraf and Caroline McClure Arraf.

(Pause.)

AMINA: I was born in Staunton Virginia. To Abdallah Ismail Arraf and Caroline McClure Arraf. I grew up between Syria and the American South.

TOM: [...]

AMINA: Neither of which was exactly the easiest place to be struggling with what I thought were inappropriate desires. When I was fifteen I realised I was gay. The thought absolutely terrified me. I was suicidal and self-destructive until I thought I'd found a way out of my sinful desires. I became what might be described by some as an Islamic extremist, by others as simply a devout Muslim.

TOM: Don't rush. They won't understand a thing.

AMINA: No longer did I have to worry about unlawful desires, but instead I could be free. I began covering my hair and suddenly found a reason to turn aside male attention. I was religious – not uninterested because of my orientation. Then I decided to join an Islamic women's devotional group. I had an older girl as a mentor. I was crazy about her. When we travelled, we would share a bed and talk hand in hand together. I was utterly devoted to her. I cried myself to sleep the day she told me she was getting married. I got older. And one day I was introduced to a suitable man and agreed to marry him. I still believed that there was something deeply wrong with me, but thought marriage would cure me. It didn't. And the marriage soon became unbearable.

TOM: You're starting to bore them.

AMINA: *(Beat.)* I came out just before my twenty-sixth birthday. *(Slowly removing the headscarf.)* First to myself, then to the woman I had fallen in love with.

TOM: That's more like it.

AMINA: For the first time in my life, I understood what it felt like to be truly liberated. But I was still living as an Arab Muslim in America. I struggled with coming out to friends and family, and so I decided to come back to Syria. I would try as hard as I could to be an openly gay woman in a repressive Arab country.

TOM: No one's going to believe you. You've got to convince them.

AMINA: It hasn't been easy. But we're here, just as we're everywhere. I went to the hair salon the other day, and as I sat there I picked up on something between the women working there. After hesitating and going around in circles for a while, I found out they were gay too. We relaxed. Talked. Laughed. Two of them were married to two gay men and lived together in Saudi Arabia. Other women came in, and I quickly realised that I was in an underground hangout. A secret dive.
Over time my eyes opened up. I soon found cafés where women held hands. We were literally everywhere.

TOM: They're going to love this.
Provoke them a little more.

AMINA: Ours is a funny country when it comes to women's rights. Our Vice President is a woman and women sit in the cabinet. Women here are far from chattel. We are not Saudi Arabia.
Many of the lesbians I know here cover up when they go out – it deters men after all. Others are among the most adamant opponents of Islamic dress. But all of us want freedom.
I chat with young women online, and more and more of them are becoming comfortable in their sexuality than I ever was. We're still a generation behind the West, but

we're catching up. We're pre-Stonewall, but we are at least halfway out of the dark. The culture here's changing. Maybe not as fast as we'd like it to, but I expect that we gain full equality here in the near future.

Maybe I'm a dreamer, but this is why I came back. I want to be a part of the change that's coming.

TOM: *(Beat.)* That's it.

WRITING AMINA

TOM: I've just posted the first two chapters of a book I'm working on. A novel – an autobiography of sorts. I'm going to go ahead and post a couple more. This whole project has been quite difficult for me. So, I'd love to hear your comments and feedback. How much to write? How much to delete? What to change to protect other people's identities?

All that kind of stuff.

TOM: Posted by Amina A. at 12:43.

CHORUS 1: Share to Twitter.

CHORUS 2: Share to Facebook.

CHORUS 3: Share to Google Buzz.

AMINA FINDS HER VOICE

CHORUS 1 joins TOM and AMINA.

TOM: *(As CHORUS 1.)* After we'd headed upstairs to my room, we kept talking about everything. What we'd do if so-and-so asked one of us to dance, or if everything went perfectly and one of us got invited by a boy to wander off.

(Pause.)

AMINA: *(To CHORUS 1.)* What then?

TOM: *(As CHORUS 1.)* Well, I guess I'd kiss him.

AMINA: *(To CHORUS 1.)* Okay. But, tell me the truth, have you ever really kissed anyone?

TOM: *(As CHORUS 1.)* Just relatives.

AMINA: *(To CHORUS 1.)* That doesn't count. I mean have you ever kissed a boy?

TOM: *(As CHORUS 1.)* No. You know you'd know. I'd have told you if I'd kissed someone over summer.
What about you?

AMINA: *(To CHORUS 1.)* Me neither. *(Beat.)* What do you think it'd be like?

TOM: *(As CHORUS 1.)* Really nice. Maybe? *(Beat.)* Well, if the boy was really cute – but, what if I made a mistake and he decided that he hated me – or made fun of me.

AMINA: *(To CHORUS 1.)* Yeah. I know. You know. I've got an idea. *(Beat.)* What if we tried out with each other? As practice. So we make sure that we're doing it right?

TOM: *(As CHORUS 1. Smiling.)* That sounds like a perfect idea. If it turns out that I'm a bad kisser, it won't count. And you won't hate me or anything. Right?

AMINA: *(To CHORUS 1.)* Of course not. You're my best friend.

TOM: *(As CHORUS 1.)* She smiled nervously and sat closer to me on my bed. Neither of us was really sure how to go about this.
(Beat.) Maybe we should be standing up?

AMINA: *(To CHORUS 1.)* I think you're supposed to close your eyes.

TOM: *(As CHORUS 1.)* I closed my eyes, tried to relax and felt her lips against mine as she bent slightly to kiss me. I remember being surprised at how soft her lips were. Warm. I felt her hands on my bare back, squeezing me closer to her.
Then she touched my breasts.
After about a minute we stopped.
'That wasn't so bad!' I laughed, and she did too.

AMINA: *(To CHORUS 1.)* You tasted nice.

TOM: *(As CHORUS 1.)* You did too. *(Beat.)* Do you know what French-kissing is?

AMINA: *(To CHORUS 1. Nodding. Beat.)* It's like with your mouth open?

TOM: *(As CHORUS 1. Nodding.)* Yeah. *(Beat.)* Maybe we should /

AMINA: *(To CHORUS 1.)* / That sounds good.

TOM: *(As CHORUS 1.)* We kept practising for a while. I remember it feeling really good. She asked me who I was thinking about and I lied and named one of the boys in our class. She laughed and said she was too.
We sat on my bed and talked – about how we'd both be really good kissers and all the boys who would want us.

(Pause.)

AMINA: *(Dreaming.)* All dark nights
And endless searches
Now are ended
At last, I have found her
The queen of all my dreaming
That source of all my longing
She has a name
A face
A voice
Now all that is left to do
Is but to win her

But that
That is the hardest part indeed
An Avernian ascent
A thousand ifs appear
And of these ifs
I have no power
All that lies within her
The true
The pure
The one
And if she scorns me?

<u>I will have been weighed in the scales</u>
<u>And found wanting</u>

(Pause.)

TOM: *(As CHORUS 1. Beat.)* As I drifted off to sleep, I remember thinking, why would I want a boyfriend if I could kiss her?

INTERROGATION

TOM: Look at me.

AMINA: […]

TOM: If you blink, we go back to the start.

AMINA: […]

TOM: Is that clear?

AMINA: Yes.

TOM: What is your name?

AMINA: Amina Abdallah Arraf Al Omari.

TOM: How old are you?

AMINA: Twenty-five.

TOM: Where are you from?

AMINA: Damascus.

TOM: Are you religious?

AMINA: Yes.

TOM: Which sect?

AMINA: […]

TOM: Which sect?

AMINA: Shia.

TOM: Have you ever had sexual intercourse?

AMINA: *(Beat.)* No.

TOM: Are you trustworthy?

AMINA: I don't understand.

TOM: Answer the question.
    Are you trustworthy?

AMINA: […]

TOM: Again.
    What is your name?

AMINA: Amina Abdallah Arraf Al Omari.

TOM: How old are you?

AMINA: Twenty-five.

TOM: Where are you from?

AMINA: Damascus.

TOM: Are you religious?

AMINA: Yes.

TOM: Which sect?

AMINA: Sunni.

TOM: Have you ever had sexual intercourse?

AMINA: […]

TOM: Again.

AMINA: Please.

TOM: I said again.
    What is your name?

AMINA: Amina Abdallah Arraf Al Omari.

TOM: How old are you?

AMINA: Twenty-five.

TOM: Where are you from?

AMINA: Damascus.

TOM: Are you religious?

AMINA: No.

TOM: Have you ever had sexual intercourse?

AMINA: […]

TOM: Have you ever had sexual intercourse?

AMINA: Yes.

(Pause.)

TOM: Are you trustworthy?

AMINA: [...]

TOM: Are you trustworthy?

(Pause.)

TOM: Again.
What is your name?

AMINA: Amina Abdallah Arraf Al Omari.

TOM: How old are you?

AMINA: Twenty-five.

TOM: Where are you from?

AMINA: Damascus.

TOM: Are you religious?

AMINA: No.

TOM: Have you ever had sexual intercourse?

AMINA: Yes.

TOM: Are you trustworthy?

AMINA: [...]

TOM: Are you trustworthy?

AMINA: No – please.
(Beat.) Please. Stop.

(Pause.)

TOM: Your eyes – your eyes just –

(Pause.)

TOM: You're the bravest girl I know.

TOM drops the needle on the record player.

Dinah Washington's 'This Bitter Earth' begins playing.

AMINA gets up and stands facing the mirror. She looks at herself intently and slowly starts to touch her face. She then puts on some make-up and lets down her hair.

TOM gently takes her by the arm and they begin to slow dance.

REVOLUTION

AMINA: Ever since the first protests began in Tunisia at the beginning of the year, people have been asking if Syria would be next. I never thought it would happen – not here. But maybe I was wrong.
Today we are mourning the first martyrs of the revolution and readying ourselves for the next stage.
A friend once told me that all good art dies after a revolution. *(Beat.)* I hope he's wrong.

FREE AMINA!

TOM: June 8th 2011.

(Pause.)

TOM: I have been on the telephone with both her parents and all we can say right now is that she is missing. Her father is desperately trying to find out where she is and who has taken her. He has asked me to share this information with her contacts.
If anyone knows anything as to her whereabouts, please contact Abdallah al Omari or please email me, Rania Ismail, at onepathtogod@gmail.com.

CHORUS 1: Post.

CHORUS 2: Like.

CHORUS 3: Repost.

CHORUS 1: Tweet.

CHORUS 2: Hashtag.

CHORUS 3: Retweet.

TOM: Amina has sent me several messages to post should something happen to her and we will wait unit we have definite word before doing so. I will post any updates as soon as I have them.

CHORUS 1: This is so painful to read. My heart goes out to this woman.

CHORUS 2: I hope they deport her. Kill her. What the fuck do I care?

CHORUS 3: I know this isn't much, but I hope her family can at least see how people all over the world care about her and pray for her release.

(Pause.)

CHORUS 1: Free Amina! Free Amina!

CHORUS 2: Free Amina!

CHORUS 3: Free Amina!

(Faster.)

*CHORUS 1: Free Amina! Free Amina! Free Amina!

*CHORUS 2: Free Amina! Free Amina! Free Amina!

*CHORUS 3: Free Amina! Free Amina! Free Amina!

(Sharp silence.)

CHORUS 1: This government feeds us nothing but lies.

CHORUS 2: Fuck those meddling Yankees.

CHORUS 3: My thoughts are with all Syrians caught up in this quest for change.

(Pause.)

CHORUS 1: On April 29th 2011, President Obama issued Executive Order 13572, imposing sanctions against persons involved in human rights abuses in Syria, and empowering the Secretary of the Treasury to further designate such persons. Three individuals and two entities were initially designated pursuant to Executive Order 13572.

A SYRIAN ROMANCE

CHORUS 3 joins TOM and AMINA.

AMINA: She looked stressed. She was still dressed from work – long cotton skirt and loose blouse.
As soon as she puts down her bag she gives me this tight hug.

TOM: *(As CHORUS 3.)* I've needed that all day.

AMINA: We sit down for dinner. I'm famished.

TOM: *(As CHORUS 3.)* There's going to be a war.
The government will want to blame someone.

AMINA: The television's on in the background. The news.
I hand her a pack of cigarettes and take one out for myself. She lights mine, then hers. She then pulls a bottle from her bag.

TOM: *(As CHORUS 3.)* Let's.

AMINA: I chew my lip for a split second.
'Sure,' I say.
I collect two glasses and let her pour – right up to the brim.

TOM: *(As CHORUS 3.)* To better days.

CHORUS 3 raises her glass.

AMINA: *(To CHORUS 3. Raising her glass.)* To better days.

(Pause.)

AMINA: We eventually settle on the couch. A rubbish soap. She soon turns off the television and starts to rub my shoulders.

TOM: *(As CHORUS 3.)* You're incredibly tense.

AMINA: Slowly, she begins to work my knotted flesh. It feels good. I begin to relax and enjoy the tension easing away. I feel her body closer to mine. Her thigh rubs against me and all I can feel is her warmth.

TOM: *(As CHORUS 3.)* How does that feel?

AMINA: I sigh as the pain from my neck releases. I say something – trying to disguise my nerves as she slides down besides me. I pull her towards me and kiss her. I feel her hands on my back squeezing me closer. My nipples tingled.

TOM: *(As CHORUS 3.)* I want to taste you.

AMINA: 'I want you too,' I say.
As I pull her shirt off over her head, we stop kissing for a moment and we just look at each other – with happiness. It's like nothing I've ever felt before.

(Pause.)

AMINA: As we fall asleep, I realise that, for the first time in my life, I'm not afraid.

HONEY TRAP

TOM: May 24th 2011.

AMINA: I received an email from Sandra the other day.

TOM: Great news! I'm in Damascus!

AMINA: I wondered when it would happen. The regime has been clamping down hard on cyber activists. I suspected it would be sooner rather than later. But still, not this soon.

TOM: I thought I'd surprise you.
(Beat.) Come to my room in the Cham Palace.
I can't wait to see you – to hold you.

AMINA: There was even a room number.
It couldn't be her. It didn't seem likely, but I still found myself hopelessly longing for her touch.
I wrote back.
'What about Laura?' I say. *(Beat.)* 'Don't you need to take her for her check-up?'

TOM: I took mum before I came. You don't need to worry about her. She's fine. The doctors gave her the all-clear.

AMINA: Wrong answer.
(Beat.) Shit. They're onto me.

I log off and shut everything down quickly.
We've had to switch our location again.

TALKING HEADS

CHORUS 1: This kidnapping is but one of many that the Syrian government has perpetrated in recent weeks.

CHORUS 2: I agree. But the Arraf case is still a unique situation. She holds dual American-Syrian citizenship and is a lesbian.

CHORUS 3: And that presents our government with a golden opportunity to take a clear stand for LGBT safety.

CHORUS 1: Absolutely. Such a statement would prove that the U.S. remains committed to freeing citizens held overseas, just as we have in North Korea and Iran.

CHORUS 2: An official declaration would also send two indispensable messages. One, that international governments must protect free speech.

CHORUS 3: And two, that democratic societies must respect LGBT equality. The government would be reiterating its tried-and-true democratic vision – free speech and protest. It's truly a no-brainer.

TOM: Her Skype message read –

*CHORUS 1: Beep beep. Tweet tweet.

*CHORUS 2: Beep beep. Tweet tweet.

*CHORUS 3: Beep beep. Tweet tweet.

CHORUS 1: Good morning. I thank you all for your patience. Ambassador Ford will now be taking questions.

CHORUS 2: I'm sure you're aware of the young Syrian American blogger, Amina Arraf, who was reportedly abducted by Syrian security forces in Damascus yesterday. What steps are your government taking to ensure her safe release?

CHORUS 3: All I can say at the moment is that we're investigating the matter. We're working to ascertain more information about Ms. Arraf, including confirmation of her citizenship.

CHORUS 2: But her cousin has already confirmed her /

CHORUS 1: / I'm sorry that's all we have time for today.

AMINA: State security searching the house.

I need to get offline.

*CHORUS 1: Beep beep. Post post.

*CHORUS 2: Beep beep. Post post.

*CHORUS 3: Beep beep. Post post.

CHORUS 1: Now back to our studio.

CHORUS 2: Thank you Dave.

This afternoon we have Sandra Bagaria with us in the studio. Ms. Bagaria is a close friend of Amina Arraf, the Syrian American blogger who was abducted by armed men in Syria on Monday night.

Thank you for being with us today.

So, when was the last time you heard from Amina?

CHORUS 3: I received an email from her about an hour before her abduction. She was going to meet with two activists from the Local Coordinating Committee.

CHORUS 2: When did you find out that she'd gone missing?

CHORUS 3: A friend in Damascus called me. He was in a complete state. Panicking. Shouting down the phone. Asking me if I knew anything about all the conflicting stories that had started coming out on Twitter.

(Beat.) I remember hanging up on him and immediately checking Amina's blog on my phone. And I saw Rania's post. I crashed to the street when I read it.

I haven't had a moment of calm since. And I haven't heard any updates about her.

It's a nightmare.

CHORUS 2: And how did she sound in that last email she sent you?

CHORUS 3: She was surprisingly upbeat. *(Beat.)* I mean she'd been having a really tough time recently. Hiding in four or five different apartments in various cities. Two young men had come to her home in Damascus several weeks before. *(Beat.)* I think they were there just following orders. They didn't seem to know what they were doing. They left without any trouble, but since that day, she believed it was only a matter of time before they would come back and arrest her.

CHORUS 2: It seems that Amina's desire to see President Bashar al-Assad fall from power drives much of her work. She's clearly a thorn in the side of the Syrian government. *(Beat.)* Did she ever mention any threats to her life before?

CHORUS 3: Well, she did think that someone was attempting to impersonate me to get close to her. She said she had received emails from me that I never wrote, telling her that I was in Damascus, and asking her to meet up. Someone had obviously hacked my email account or somehow pretended to be me. They were trying to approach her, I think.

CHORUS 2: In one of her last posts before going into hiding she wrote, 'the Syria I always hoped was there, but was sleeping, has woken up. I have to believe that, sooner or later, we will prevail.' *(Beat.)* Are other activists you're in touch with equally optimistic about this protest movement and a democratic future for Syria?

CHORUS 3: Amina has always maintained that, despite everything that was happening to her, she would never flee Syria. She and other activists are sacrificing their lives for a more open and free country.

CHORUS 2: The risks faced by Syrian activists armed only with mobile phones and Internet connections are made plain in this chilling clip posted online just after Amina's arrest. *(A shaky low-quality camera phone video begins playing in the background.)* According to the Anonymous Syria Twitter feed, this video was recorded by an activist who was shot dead while filming tanks shelling Talbiseh, just outside the city of Homs.

AMINA: I think they've gone.
Wait.

*CHORUS 1: Beep beep. Tweet tweet.

*CHORUS 2: Beep beep. Tweet tweet.

*CHORUS 3: Beep beep. Tweet tweet.

CHORUS 1: We're a global web movement to bring people-powered politics to decision-making everywhere.

CHORUS 2: A transnational community. Democratic.

CHORUS 3: More effective than the United Nations.

CHORUS 1: Our online community can act like a megaphone to call attention to important issues.

CHORUS 2: It's a lightning rod to channel public concern into specific, targeted campaigns.

CHORUS 3: A stem cell that grows into whatever form of advocacy is best suited to meet our most urgent needs.

AMINA: My laptop battery's dying.
If not online tomorrow, I'm dead or arrested.

*CHORUS 1: Beep beep. Post post.

*CHORUS 2: Beep beep. Post post.

*CHORUS 3: Beep beep. Post post.

CHORUS 1: It's all about breaking the Middle East blackout.

CHORUS 2: Funded by generous donations from over 30,000 members, our team is working closely with the leadership of democracy movements in Syria to get them high-tech phones and satellite Internet modems, connect them to the world's top media outlets, and provide communications advice.

CHORUS 3: We've seen the power of this engagement – where our support to activists has created global media cycles with footage and eyewitness accounts that our team helps distribute to CNN, BBC, Al Jazeera and other channels. *(Beat.)* The courage of these activists is unbelievable.

(Pause.)

CHORUS 1: Secretary Clinton. Over here.

CHORUS 2: Over here.

CHORUS 1: Over here.

CHORUS 2: Over here.

CHORUS 1: Secretary Clinton.

CHORUS 2: Secretary of State. What do you make of the Syrian government's decision to shutdown local Internet servers?

CHORUS 3: We condemn any effort to suppress the Syrian people's exercise of their rights to free expression, assembly and association.

TOM: It's okay. She's safe.

*CHORUS 1: Beep beep. Like like.

*CHORUS 2: Beep beep. Like like.

*CHORUS 3: Beep beep. Like like.

(Pause.)

*TOM: Is this dawn or dusk? *(Beat.)* The winds of change are blowing hard across the Middle East. In just a few short weeks, regimes that have seemed immune from change have been toppled by mass uprisings, first in Tunisia, then in Egypt. While the name Tahrir suddenly seems familiar, new mass uprisings clamour for our attention – Libya, Algeria, Bahrain, Yemen, Jordan and even Iraq. Instead of the usual depressing stories, these countries are now in the news as examples of bravery and commitment to freedom and democracy. From where I sit, here in Damascus, one of the few quiet and stable places in the region, it feels like a fresh wind of freedom is sweeping away the tired and old dictatorships. We are, we feel, at the heart of a revolution. We hope that these changes will mean a real blossoming of freedom. We're ready. We've been waiting for this moment. But we also hear voices from beyond the region telling us that, instead of freedom, we should be scared. Those kings and dictators may be bad, but the alternative is far worse, they tell us. Instead of these tired and compromised despots, they say, we will have new dictators. They warn us of Islamic fundamentalists just waiting to seize power and deny us our freedom.

*AMINA: <u>Is this dawn or dusk?</u> *(Beat.)* <u>The winds of change are blowing hard across the Middle East. In just a few short weeks, regimes that have seemed immune from change have been toppled by mass uprisings, first in Tunisia, then in Egypt. While the name Tahrir suddenly seems familiar, new mass uprisings clamour for our attention – Libya, Algeria, Bahrain, Yemen, Jordan and even Iraq. Instead of the usual depressing stories, these countries are now in the news as examples of bravery and commitment to freedom and democracy. From where I sit, here in Damascus, one of the few quiet and stable places in the region, it feels like a fresh wind of freedom is sweeping away the tired and old dictatorships. We are, we feel, at the heart of a revolution. We hope that these changes will mean a real blossoming of freedom. We're ready. We've been waiting for this moment. But we also hear voices from beyond the region telling us that, instead of freedom, we should be scared. Those kings and dictators may be bad, but the alternative is far worse, they tell us. Instead of these tired and compromised despots, they say, we will have new dictators. They warn us of Islamic fundamentalists just waiting to seize power and deny us our freedom.</u>

TOM: Posted by Amina A. at 16:32.

CHORUS 1: Share to Twitter.

CHORUS 2: Share to Facebook.

CHORUS 3: Share to Google Buzz.

WHO'S THAT GIRL?

CHORUS 1: Login. Username. At acarvin.

Password.

New message.

CHORUS 2: Just wanted to ask again full stop. Has anyone met hashtag Amina open bracket Gay Girl in Damascus close bracket in person question mark. If so comma, please contact me full stop.

CHORUS 1: Reply.

CHORUS 2: Retweet.

CHORUS 3: Favourite.

THE MONEY SHOT

Haifa Wehbe's 'Ragab' is playing.

CHORUS 3 joins TOM and AMINA.

TOM gets up and violently moves AMINA in her chair.

CHORUS 3 sits in the other chair opposite AMINA.

(Long pause.)

TOM: Spread your legs.

AMINA hesitates.

TOM: I said spread your legs.

AMINA hesitates and then slowly opens her legs.

TOM: Wider.

AMINA: […]

TOM: Wider.

AMINA slowly opens her legs wider and looks up at TOM.

TOM: Don't fucking look at me.

AMINA: […]

TOM: Touch yourself.

AMINA: […]

TOM: Touch yourself, I said.

> *AMINA unzips and slowly puts her hand in her trousers. A tear rolls down her cheek.*

TOM: *(Closing his eyes.)* Slowly.

> *(Pause.)*

TOM: Slower.

> *(Pause.)*

TOM: Deeper.

> *(Pause.)*

TOM: Deeper.

> *AMINA begins to breathe deeply as tears start to stream down her face.*
>
> *(Pause.)*

AMINA: *(To CHORUS 3.)* What's your name?

CHORUS 3: Paula.

TOM: *(To AMINA.)* Kiss her. *(Beat.)* I want to see you kiss.

AMINA BECOMES AN INTERNATIONAL FIGURE

TOM: April 25th 2011.

> My father, the hero.

AMINA: We had a visit from the security services. It was late at night. Everyone was fast asleep. Abu Ali, our doorman, was woken up by someone ringing at the gate. He stumbled outside to take a look and saw two young men in their early twenties, clad in black leather jackets, muscular and both smoking. He knew immediately who they were and rang the alarm. He was surprised when they said that they'd come for me.

As soon as I woke up, I knew exactly what was happening. I pulled on my clothes as fast as I could. The ones I had prepared for this moment. Simple cotton underwear – no underwire or anything like that – a T-shirt, jeans and a loose-fitting pullover.

When I got downstairs, my father was already outside. He was standing there in his nightshirt – arguing with the two men. When I appeared, one of them nodded –

TOM: That's her.

AMINA: Me?

TOM: Yes. You.

AMINA: He rattles off a long list of things I'd posted online. *(Beat.)* 'You might have missed a few,' I say. My nerves almost getting the worst of me. I suddenly have this urge to flee. I clamp down hard. *(Beat.)* If I run, I know they'll shoot. I look at their weapons, the bulge of pistols and knives under their jackets.

TOM: We have enough. Conspiring against the state, supporting an armed uprising, working with foreign elements.

AMINA: Who?

TOM: The Salafis. Making sectarian plots –

AMINA: 'Really?' My father interrupts. 'My daughter's a Salafi?' *(Beat.)* 'Look at her.' They say nothing.

(Pause.)

AMINA: 'I didn't think so.' *(Beat.)* 'When was the last time you heard one of them saying there should be no state religion?'

(Pause.)

AMINA: Nothing.

(Pause.)

AMINA: 'When was the last time you saw them saying homosexuals should be allowed the right to marry?'

(Pause.)

AMINA: Nothing.

(Pause.)

AMINA: 'And when you say nothing, you show that you have no reason to take my daughter away from me.'

(Pause.)

AMINA: Nothing. They say nothing. Then one whispers something to the other. *(Beat.)* He smiles.

TOM: *(Beat.)* And your daughter tells you everything does she?

AMINA: 'Of course.'

TOM: Did she tell you that she likes women? *(Beat.)* That she's one of those faggots that likes to fuck little girls?

AMINA: 'She's my daughter. And she's who she is. If you want her, you'll have to take me as well.'

TOM: *(Laughing.)* You stupid fuck. No wonder she ended up fucking dykes and kikes.

AMINA: He steps towards me and puts his hand on my breast. I hold my breath.

TOM: Maybe if you were a real man you'd stop all this nonsense. Maybe we should show you now, so you understand how real men are.

AMINA: My dad whispers something in my ear. *(Beat.)* I can't quite make it out.

(Pause.)

AMINA: 'No. You'll leave her alone and tell the rest of your gang to do the same. We're Sunni. You know that. And in your offices and villages they're telling you that all of you must stand shoulder to shoulder now because we're coming for you as soon as we can, and we'll serve you as they have served ours in the land of the two rivers. So you're scared. I would be too. You've come here to take Amina. *(Beat.)* Let me tell you something. She's not the one you should fear. Your Bashar and your Maher, they'll not live forever, they'll not rule forever, and you both know that. So, you'll not be taking Amina away from here. You'll go back and you'll tell the rest of your gang not to come here again.'

(Long pause.)

TOM: [...] *(Nodding.)* Go back to sleep.

(Pause.)

AMINA: As soon as the gate shut all I could hear was thunderous applause. Everyone in the house was awake by now and had been watching from their balconies, doorways and windows. All around the courtyard everyone was cheering. My dad had defeated them! My dad had defeated them! And not with weapons, but with words. I hugged and kissed him. This time we'd won. So, when my father says he'll not leave until either democracy comes or he is dead, I have no choice but to stay. Not because he's making me, but because he isn't. We sent the rest away. Anyone who could left for Beirut. I can't go. He's staying. *(Beat.)* And so will I.

TOM: Posted by Amina A. at 13:05.

CHORUS 1: Share to Twitter.

CHORUS 2: Share to Facebook.

CHORUS 3: Share to Google Buzz.

TOM smiles.

Kanye West's 'Flashing Lights' begins playing.

A sudden avalanche of flash photography.

*CHORUS 1: Flashing. Lights.

*CHORUS 2: Flashing. Lights.

*CHORUS 3: Flashing. Lights.

*CHORUS 1: Flashing. Lights.

*CHORUS 2: Flashing. Lights.

*CHORUS 3: Flashing. Lights.

*CHORUS 1: Flashing. Lights.

*CHORUS 2: Flashing. Lights.

*CHORUS 3: Flashing. Lights.

*CHORUS 1: Flashing. Lights.

*CHORUS 2: Flashing. Lights.

*CHORUS 3: Flashing. Lights.

*CHORUS 4: Flashing. Lights.

Blackout.

MY FATHER'S DAUGHTER

TOM: May 3ʳᵈ 2011.

> *CHORUS 2 joins TOM and AMINA.*

AMINA: So, now our house is empty. My mother and the rest of the family are gone. After the Mukhabarat [intelligence service] came, they left to Beirut. They're not the only ones to leave these last few days. Many of those of who can afford to have slipped out of the country. I can't really blame them for leaving. I would probably leave too if it were just me.

> *(Pause.)*

> *CHORUS 2 holds up a backgammon set.*

TOM: *(As CHORUS 2.)* Shall we?

AMINA: *(To CHORUS 2.)* Yes.

TOM: *(As CHORUS 2.)* You sure? *(Beat.)* What was the score last time?

AMINA: *(To CHORUS 2.)* Okay baba.

> *AMINA begins setting up the game.*

> *CHORUS 2 collects an old bottle with a ripped label and sits down opposite AMINA.*

> *CHORUS 2 pours himself a glass.*

TOM: *(As CHORUS 2.)* Do you want?

AMINA: *(To CHORUS 2. Nodding.)* […]

> *CHORUS 2 adds an ice cube and then a little water to each glass.*

TOM: *(As CHORUS 2.)* Cheers.

CHORUS 2 raises his glass.

AMINA: *(To CHORUS 2. Raising her glass.)* Cheers.

(Pause.)

AMINA: We carry on drinking through the night.
We start running over all the possibilities. The shared fate
of our country.

(Pause.)

AMINA: *(Taking another swig.)* Round two.
He shows me a photo of his grandfather.

TOM: *(As CHORUS 2. Holding a photo.)* Now that's a real man. If
we'd won the Great War, we wouldn't be in this mess. All
the British and French ever did was stab us in the back.
We never learn.

(Pause.)

AMINA: *(Taking another swig.)* Round three. We're both drunk
by now.

TOM: *(As CHORUS 2.)* Whose go is it?

AMINA: *(To CHORUS 2.)* I don't know baba.

TOM: *(As CHORUS 2.)* Mine.

(Pause.)

AMINA: I remind him that he once served the regime.

TOM: *(As CHORUS 2.)* By making sure that people lived. I was
an engineer – not a killer.

(Pause.)

TOM: *(As CHORUS 2.)* Why did you agree to marry Hisham?
Your mother and I. *(Beat.)* We both knew you were gay.

(Pause.)

AMINA: *(To CHORUS 2.)* You let me. You never –
I didn't want to disappoint you.

REQUEST FOR READERS

TOM: So, as I posted previously, I'm writing this autobiographical novel. I've uploaded bits of it on this blog. I'm thinking I should probably find an agent. *(Beat.)* Anyone out there know one?
Please comment below.

(Pause.)

TOM: Posted by Amina A. at 16:06.

CHORUS 1: Share to Twitter.

CHORUS 2: Share to Facebook.

CHORUS 3: Share to Google Buzz.

PINKWASHING

TOM: I feared that this day would come.
I received a request from a reporter at CNN who was preparing a piece on gay rights and the Arab Spring. I had my doubts. I knew they'd try and pull the sort of pinkwashing that enemies of Arab freedom have come to rely on. But I went ahead with it.
I don't regret anything I said.

CHORUS 1: So, will gays be sacrificial lambs in the Arab Spring?

CHORUS 2: Well, it's difficult to say really. The uprisings bringing political change and demonstrations across much of the Arab world have given millions of people hope of greater freedom.
Equally some gay people in the Middle East fear exactly the opposite.

CHORUS 3: That isn't strictly the case. Some have a far more positive view of the situation in Syria. A Syrian woman who writes a blog called 'A Gay Girl in Damascus' says she returned to Syria last year after many years in the United States. In an email interview Abdallah said she believed that political change could improve gay rights.

TOM: A whole lot of long-time changes are suddenly bubbling to the surface and views towards women, gay people and minorities are changing rapidly. What has really startled me has been the fact that I've received no criticism from Islamic sources. It's sort of indicative of the sea change that's happened here – suddenly people are working together, regardless of their other views, to achieve a single goal – a free Syria.

CHORUS 1: Not everyone shares Abdallah's optimism though. Dan Littauer, the London-based editor of Gay Middle East, told us –

CHORUS 2: Many gay activists are very scared that the reality of their oppression could get worse.
As long as religion has a big impact on governments around the Arab world, it'll always be this way.

CHORUS 3: I have to agree with Dan there. In Egypt and Tunisia there was a lot of hope initially that there would be a more tolerant civil society. Now it seems that the impetus for change will be hijacked by conservative forces who'll make the situation worse for gay people and other minorities.

AMINA: I warned you Tom. I told you about their insatiable appetite for the moor. What did I say? *(Beat.)* That they would try and divide us. Conquer us. That rhetoric. Turning gay rights into a weapon of imperialism. A logic that advocates war, occupation and dispossession. It's a final justification for genocide.

(Pause.)

AMINA: Page for page you say that we're born equal. But heroes don't exist Tom. Not in our world. This world. I've seen the future and it doesn't belong to your kind. No. You're hollow. Obsolete. Poisonous.

THE 'ARAB AWAKENING'

TOM: May 21st 2011.

(Pause.)

TOM: Our Arab Spring is finally underway!

(Pause.)

TOM: Posted by Amina A. at 19:26.

CHORUS 1: Share to Twitter.

CHORUS 2: Share to Facebook.

CHORUS 3: Share to Google Buzz.

TROLLING

CHORUS 1: We've gathered compelling new evidence regarding the Gay Girl in Damascus blogger. Those responsible have caused a great deal of concern and anguish by posting information alleging that Amina Abdallah Arraf al Omari had been kidnapped from the streets of Damascus.

CHORUS 2: A measure of the concern that this story has caused is the formation of a Facebook group with more than 15,000 members.

CHORUS 3: We believe that the person or persons responsible should end this deception, which has been harmful to individuals who trusted and believed in Amina and has sown confusion at a time when real people are in danger in Syria and in other countries in the region.

CHORUS 1: We don't know the motive of the person or persons behind the hoax. The information presented connects the Amina blogger to two real people.

*CHORUS 1: Thomas J MacMaster and Britta Froelicher.

*CHORUS 2: Thomas J MacMaster and Britta Froelicher.

*CHORUS 3: Thomas J MacMaster and Britta Froelicher.

(Pause.)

CHORUS 1: We wrote to MacMaster, requesting to speak to him about Amina, to which he responded –

TOM: Thanks, but as I have stated before, it's neither Britta nor I.

CHORUS 2: A follow-up email presenting the information we'd uncovered was met with the following response –

TOM: Unfortunately, we're on vacation, so I wouldn't be able to do so. We've already been confronted by the *Washington Post* with these allegations and have denied them and will continue to do so.

CHORUS 3: And his final response –

TOM: I'm not the blogger in question. Whoever that person really is, I have doubtless interacted with her at some point. I don't know anything more about her. When I first read the news story, I momentarily thought I had an idea who she was. As time has progressed that seems much less likely. I understand there are a number of unusual coincidences regarding the blogger and both me and my wife. Those are, as far as I am aware, simply unusual. I'm not going to make more of that.

CHORUS 1: On a private Yahoo discussion group named 'the crescent land' that was run and operated by Amina, and has since been closed down, the following name and address were displayed –

TOM: Amina Arraf and Ian Lazarus. c/o Mr & Mrs Abdallah Arraf-Omari. 5646 Crestwood Drive. SW Stone Mountain, GA 30087.

CHORUS 2: But there is no evidence of an Amina Arraf, Ian Lazarus or Mr and Mrs Abdallah Arraf-Omari ever owning or occupying this address.

CHORUS 3: According to State of Georgia property records, the house at that address was owned by Thomas MacMaster.

*CHORUS 1: By sharing this information, we want to provide the best chance that this story can be brought to closure and people's attention directed back toward real world events.

*CHORUS 2: By sharing this information, we want to provide the best chance that this story can be brought to closure and people's attention directed back toward real world events.

*CHORUS 3: By sharing this information, we want to provide the best chance that this story can be brought to closure and people's attention directed back toward real world events.

*CHORUS 1: Beep beep. Tweet tweet.

*CHORUS 2: Beep beep. Tweet tweet.

*CHORUS 3: Beep beep. Tweet tweet.

(Pause.)

TOM: I've received a good bit of mail and attention these past two weeks. Most of it has been wonderful. I wish I had the time to send personal thanks to every single person who has been so awesomely nice to me – sent me good thoughts and reposted what's happening here in Syria. Thank you. But there have also been messages and comments that have left me sick to my stomach. The hate. It's a sickness. I've tried so hard to ignore them – this brave new world of trolls. I know they're coming from the Mukhabarat and their lackeys who simply toe the regime line. The war's no longer just in the streets. The Internet is the new frontline. They've got hackers working day and night trying to shut us down and expose us. They're hacking Facebook and other social media – spewing regime propaganda.

TOM: Posted by Amina A. at 08:49.

SERVER NOT FOUND

AMINA: June 3rd 2011.

(Pause.)

AMINA: The first authorised demonstration was supposed to take place today. A candlelight vigil for all our dead. But the regime decided to rescind the permit this morning. We continue our struggle /

TOM: Amina /

AMINA: The day's coming – and when it comes, we will win /

TOM: Amina /

AMINA: Fatherland or death! We will win!

TOM: Amina. Look at me when I'm talking to you. *(Beat.)* Hey. Answer me. *(Beat.)* You've become a cruel woman. You're nothing without me. *(Beat.)* You hear me? Nothing. Insignificant. Your little revolt. *(Beat.)* A joke. It's utterly meaningless. You'll fade to black without me. You need me.

AMINA: Not anymore.

(Pause.)

TOM: June 3rd 2011.

(Pause.)

TOM: As of last night, the Syrian government has shut down all Internet service inside Syria. As far as we know, Amina is unable to update her blog. As soon as we hear more, we will share it.

(Pause.)

TOM: Posted by Rania at 18:22.

CHORUS 1: Share to Twitter.

CHORUS 2: Share to Facebook.

CHORUS 3: Share to Google Buzz.

TOM STANDS FIRM

TOM: Istanbul.
  June 12th 2011.

AMINA: Apology to readers.

TOM: I never expected this level of attention. While the
  narrative voice may have been fictional, the facts of this
  blog are true and not misleading as to the situation on the
  ground. I don't believe that I've harmed anyone. I feel
  that I've created an important voice for issues that I feel
  strongly about.
  I only hope that everyone pays as much attention to the
  people of the Middle East and their struggles in this year
  of revolutions. The events there are being shaped by the
  people living them on a daily basis. I have only tried to
  illuminate them for a Western audience.
  This experience has sadly only confirmed my feelings
  regarding the often superficial coverage of the Middle East
  and the pervasiveness of new forms of liberal Orientalism.
  (Beat.) However, I have been deeply touched by the
  reactions of readers.

TOM: The sole author of all posts on this blog.
  Posted by Amina A. at 16:47.

CHORUS 1: Share to Twitter.

CHORUS 2: Share to Facebook.

CHORUS 3: Share to Google Buzz.

TOM'S FACEBOOK FRIENDS

*CHORUS 1: Status update.

*CHORUS 2: Status update.

*CHORUS 3: Status update.

TOM: I'm quite possibly a contender for worst person in the
  world.

*CHORUS 1: Comment.

*CHORUS 2: Comment.

*CHORUS 3: Comment.

CHORUS 1: I'm glad you're finally being recognised for your writing.

TOM: Thumbs up.

*CHORUS 1: Comment.

*CHORUS 2: Comment.

*CHORUS 3: Comment.

CHORUS 2: I do hope that besides the attention you've brought to light on several different political and social issues, that you actually get to profit in some way from your efforts.

TOM: Thumbs up.

*CHORUS 1: Comment.

*CHORUS 2: Comment.

*CHORUS 3: Comment.

CHORUS 3: You likely inspired compassion for an otherwise oppressed population. Be gentle and compassionate to yourself Tom.

TOM: Thumbs up.

*CHORUS 1: Comment.

*CHORUS 2: Comment.

*CHORUS 3: Comment.

CHORUS 1: This whole incident is starting to make me think that maybe I shouldn't have given that Nigerian prince my bank account information. Nah, I'm sure it's fine.

TOM: Thumbs up.

CHORUS 2: Thumbs up.

CHORUS 3: Thumbs /

*CHORUS 1: / Comment removed.

*CHORUS 2: / Comment removed.

*CHORUS 3: / Comment removed.

(Pause.)

Chorus 2 Do you understand the depth of the situation? *(Beat.)*
I'm not sure – I'm afraid you may one day. Just think –
take people who don't know you personally, then they
hear you may want to write a novel.

(Pause.)

CHORUS 3: This has been flagged as spam.

THE REVOLUTION WILL BE TELEVISED

AMINA: The whole country has arisen!
If you have more videos, please post them in the
comments.

TOM: It's been a while. I miss you. You know I'd never try to
hurt you. You're everything I am.
Just promise me you'll be careful. That's all I ask of you.
I pray that you forgive me.

RITUAL

AMINA: It's still far from over. We have new rituals now. New
rites of ablution. I keep my nails trimmed shorter than
before. I clip my father's toenails and we dye each other's
hair. I keep my nails trimmed shorter than before. I clip
my father's toenails and we dye each other's hair. We write
our names, our identity numbers and phone numbers
every Friday before prayers. We write our names, our
identity numbers and phone numbers every Friday before
prayers. I write it all out clearly in both English and Arabic
on my father's back and chest – and he does the same for
me.
Because when we're dead, once they've washed us down
and wrapped us in white sheets, I want to be sure that
people know who we were – our names and what became
of us.

JELENA SPEAKS

A blown-up profile photo of Jelena Lecic adorns the wall.

Jeremy Paxman's Newsnight discussion with Jelena Lecic and Mahmoud Hammad is projected and plays out in full (broadcast on Wednesday 8 June 2011).

Jelena's blown-up profile photo starts to disintegrate, then reform and morph into something indistinguishable – something utterly revolting.

(Pause.)

CHORUS 1: This is the same girl who made a false testimony to convince the US to enter Kuwait during the Persian Gulf War.

CHORUS 2: Go to this link.

CHORUS 3: Damn. Nice looking babe. LOL. The lib-Muslim wet dream Amina Gay Girl in Damascus doesn't exist and is actually a bearded straight man in Britain.

CHORUS 1: Americans are dumbass hicks. I can't believe they think they can get away with this shit.

CHORUS 2: May China rape the US

CHORUS 3: May China rape the US?

CHORUS 1: You really are an idiot.

CHORUS 2: If you can't see past the fake picture, then you're dumb. Read *An Inspector Calls*, Inspector Ghoul comes out and corrects all these social wrongs amongst this corrupt family, but it turns out that he wasn't even a real Inspector. So the old snobbish members of that family then dismiss the advice from Ghoul, whereas the younger generation take his advice anyway and change for the better. Don't take it at face value. This happens in other countries.

CHORUS 3: The guy keeps being like 'isn't this a cautionary tale'. And both of them are kinda like – meh. No, this is not a 'cautionary tale' that you should not post normal face photos online. Sorry, asshole, stop blaming the victim.

CHORUS 1: Surely people can understand the reasons behind Amina not using her own photo. In her defense, she probably started off not knowing how popular she'd eventually become, but it wasn't a smart move.

CHORUS 2: <u>Jelena comes across as a complete dick.</u>

CHORUS 1: A complete –

CHORUS 2: <u>Dick.</u>

CHORUS 3: If Amina and her story are real, then I hope Jelena looks back at this interview and is ashamed at her stroppy behaviour over a minor inconvenience.

CHORUS 1: The Syrian blogger who defends 'Amina' must feel like an idiot now.

CHORUS 2: So, turns out it's some Turkish guy. Not surprising – these guys are kinda feminine.

CHORUS 3: Amina doesn't exist, and if she does she's a fucking bitch for ruining someone else's life.

*CHORUS 1: Comment removed.

*CHORUS 2: Comment removed.

*CHORUS 3: Comment removed.

CHORUS 1: Exposed. Syrian peace activist is a CIA propagandist. Go to this link.

CHORUS 2: I'm also a lesbian, but I'm trapped in a man's body. Winning.

*CHORUS 1: This has been flagged as spam.

*CHORUS 2: This has been flagged as spam.

*CHORUS 3: This has been flagged as spam.

CHORUS 3: This is a stupid attempt to get liberals on board with bombing Syria. It's a slight of hand to distract from the fact that the Syrian opposition is full of Islamists who liberals won't support.

CHORUS 1: Too many people with too much time on their sticky fingers.

CHORUS 2: This is all so postmodern.

CHORUS 3: <u>Amina's fit.</u>

CHORUS 2: Amina's –

CHORUS 1: *(Beat.)* Who cares. We both like pussy.

CHORUS 2: I'd do her.

CHORUS 3: How is this newsworthy?

A FALSE PROPHET

TOM takes duct tape and tapes AMINA's mouth.

(Pause.)

AMINA struggles violently to speak to TOM over CHORUS.

CHORUS 1: People desperately wanted to believe in this hero. A saucy, sage, left-wing member of the LGBT community who likes to wear the hijab, can't stand Israel or George W. Bush, and who parrots every cliché about the romantic authenticity of the Arab people and their poetic yearning for democracy, peace, and love.

CHORUS 2: MacMaster's fake-but-accurate lesbian was perfectly pitched to Western liberals desperate to alleviate the pain of cognitive dissonance. No longer must you think too hard or make tough choices if you're, say, anti-Israel and pro-democracy, or pro-gay rights and in favour of the self- determination of Muslim fanatics.

CHORUS 3: Heck, you can even stop worrying and love a lesbian feminist who sees no big deal in wearing a religiously required sack over her head. With Amina, all contradictions are resolved – in favour of the incoherent biases of the anti-America and anti-Israel Left.

AMINA finally relents.

CHORUS 1: His irresponsible stunt has done nothing for gays, and nothing for those revolting against oppressive regimes in the Middle East.

CHORUS 2: Not only that. He's provided ample grist to the mill of those who would dearly love to re-brand all progressive forces in the region as willing tools of the US

CHORUS 3: Come on, this was not just a stupid hoax –
it's obvious that he was paid to do this by the Syrian
government to discredit all future protests.

CHORUS 1: Tom MacMaster is a spook. And so is his wife.
They're bought and paid for by the CIA, or some other
alphabet soup agency, whose real goal is to get the Russian
navy out of Syria. It's the same Zbigniew Brzezinski
doctrine they used during the Carter administration to get
the Soviets into Afghanistan.

CHORUS 2: I remember hearing that before. *(Beat.)* Where did
you get that? Was it from *Family Guy* or *American Dad*?

CHORUS 3: Oh, by the way I'm King William III and I'm
selling one of my private tropical islands for $15 million.
What a deal. Please contact me if you wish to buy it.

*CHORUS 1: This has been flagged as spam.

*CHORUS 2: This has been flagged as spam.

*CHORUS 3: This has been flagged as spam.

CHORUS 3: What a typical liberal moron.

THE 'ARAB SPRING'

Kanye West's 'Gold Digger' is playing.

The CHORUS sing the refrain from 'Gold Digger'.

*TOM picks up a pair of scissors and a brown paper bag. He cuts holes for
the eyes and mouth. He then places the bag on his head.*

AMINA puts on a balaclava and headset.

CHORUS 1: Support Tom MacMaster.
AKA Gay Girl Damascus.

CHORUS 2: Don't vilify the guy just because you're ashamed
and didn't realise he was a man. It's irrelevant who or
where he was based. As an activist he was achieving his
goals and your goals.

The sound of a Skype dial tone.

AMINA: I'd like to say to the American people. The same way you like freedom and democracy, and to live in security. We're no different. We're human beings.

CHORUS 3: Resistance is *always* possible. But we must engage in resistance first of all by developing the idea of a technological culture. The ideals of technological culture remain underdeveloped and therefore outside of popular culture and the practical ideals of democracy.

CHORUS 1: In fact you supported him because he gave voice where there was silence. Who cares about his identity? It's funny, but you do. Why stone him in the village centre when you claim to represent tolerance and dialogue?

CHORUS 2: Who are you to say what is authentic and what is not? Who are you to say who is authentic and who is not? You're using identity politics in a completely hypocritical manner.

CHORUS 3: This is why society as a whole has no control over technological developments. And this is one of the gravest threats to democracy in the near future. It's imperative to develop a democratic technological culture.

AMINA: We deliberately film crowds from a distance so individuals can't be recognised or arrested. We also use encryption software given to us by the US State Department that prevents the government from tracking the video's source. After we send the videos we immediately erase the hard drive.

CHORUS 1: To Tom MacMaster, the Gay Girl in Damascus, right on you!

CHORUS 2: Many of us are employing the same techniques for the same reasons. Don't let them get you down.

CHORUS 3: I believe that these three revolutions lead to a technical essentialism – a cybercult. Just as there's religious, there's a technical essentialism through technical fundamentalism. *(Beat.)* And it's just as frightening as religious fundamentalism.

AMINA: They said, 'will you continue writing this nonsense?'
I said, if I see something wrong, I will write about it. I will
not be silent. Then they said, in a cold-blooded way, okay,
cool, we will help you to stop writing. They put my hand
on the table and they broke it.
(Smiling.) The people are determined to take the regime
out.

AN AMERICAN WINTER

TOM removes the paper bag.

*AMINA slowly removes the balaclava, puts on the headscarf, tucks in her
hair and carefully rearranges it.*

TOM begins to pour black ink slowly down his face.

AMINA: Those mountains of facts will tell you what, exactly?
They were born, they lived, they died – and what does that
show? It explains nothing, reveals nothing and says only
that we have ancestors and we're related to other people.
That you and I are probably cousins somehow, and that
you have other cousins and, if you traced far enough back,
you could show that every one of us was endlessly related
and that we were all cousins and what would it matter?

TOM: Did your face just change?

AMINA: <u>What?</u>

TOM: Just now. Your face. I didn't recognise it.

AMINA: <u>My face?</u>

TOM: I thought it changed?

AMINA: <u>What do you mean?</u>

TOM: I thought it became someone else's. Your eyes changed.
Your lips felt – *(Beat.)* For a moment I didn't recognise you.

AMINA: <u>Listen to me now.</u> It's important that you listen. <u>You
must never say a word about me to anyone you ever meet.</u>
From this moment on, for the rest of your life, you must
never shut your eyes.

69

TOM: No – no. Please. No. I don't understand /

AMINA: <u>/ In this place, the land of the left hand, when you see those images inside your head, I want you to burn them.</u>

TOM: I won't let you. You can't just – what do you think you're /

AMINA: / Revolutions aren't born. They're made – created from something else. Something more earthly.
The universe always needs things to fall into place. Broken parts that can be put back into place, fixed, the way they once were. The way they should be. *(Beat.)* But it's not the same with people. Some things can't be corrected. They must remain as they are. Damaged.

(Pause.)

CHORUS 1: They're nothing but words in a story.

CHORUS 2: I never met her.

CHORUS 3: They're nothing but words in a story.

CHORUS 1: I never met her.

CHORUS 2: They're nothing but words in a story.

CHORUS 3: I never met her.

CHORUS 1: They're nothing but words in a story.

CHORUS 2: I never met her.

CHORUS 3: They're nothing but words in a story.

CHORUS 1: I never met her.

CHORUS 2: They're nothing but words in a story.

CHORUS 3: I never met her.

CHORUS 1: They're nothing but words in a story.

CHORUS 2: I never met her.

CHORUS 3: They're nothing but words in a story.

The CHORUS exit.

HERO

AMINA: For far too long now I've been living a dream that hasn't belonged to me. My eyes. If you had my eyes – the things you would see. This isn't a fairytale or an Arabian night's tale. This is a history of everything that happened. If you read the mainstream press, you'll know that it's axiomatic that Arabs are unreliable and prone to lying. So, if you buy that reasoning, then you should expect me to lie at every turn. *(Beat.)* I promise you I won't, but really, will it matter?

This is a true story, so, to my eternal regret, a fairytale ending won't do. If you've come to help me, you're wasting your time. But if you've come because your liberation is bound up with mine, then let us work together in solidarity.

I probably don't have much more time, but I'll never fade away.

Promise me one thing. *(Beat.)* That you'll sing about me.

ANTIHERO

TOM: Sometimes. When she wakes up, I don't know what mood she might be in. Some days she's fine. Others – Sometimes she'd wake up happy like a baby phoenix. Sometimes she'd be so sad she'd want to spend time alone. It was like she'd be pushing her fingers down her throat to point at her heart. I could see her working at her smiles. But the sadness was still there. Anyone could see it. Smiles take work. And I know her life has been hard. But with the smell of coffee on her breath, she'd say we'll make it. Two of us for tomorrow. I can't help though, for the sorrow is stronger than the pain.

It's all scorched earth now.

(Pause.)

TOM: Did I tell you how beautiful you look tonight?
All I want is to see me in your eyes again.

TOM drops the needle on the record player.

Dinah Washington's 'This Bitter Earth' begins playing.

TOM: *(Reaching out to AMINA.)* Sweetheart.

AMINA doesn't move.

TOM: Please.

AMINA remains still.

TOM: Put your arm around me.

(Long pause.)

AMINA: It's beautiful.

TOM: What is?

AMINA: This life.
Even on the eve of death, it's never too late to start again.

LETTING GO

Asmahan's 'When Will You Realise?' is playing.

AMINA picks up a hand mirror.

TOM turns and AMINA holds up the mirror in his direction.

TOM takes out a pocket comb, combs his hair and fixes himself up as he looks in the mirror.

TOM: Istanbul. June 13th 2011.

AMINA: Apology to readers.

TOM: […]

(Pause.)

TOM: Statement regarding the Gay Girl in Damascus blog.

(Pause.)

AMINA sing's Ashmahan's 'When Will You Realise' to underscore TOM's apology.

*TOM: I – I'm the sole author of this blog and have always been so. Any and all posts on the blog are by me.
Before I say anything else, I want to apologise to anyone

I may have hurt or harmed in any way. I never meant to hurt anyone. Words alone do not suffice to express how badly I feel about all this. I betrayed the trust of a great many people, the friendship that was honestly and openly offered to me, and played with the emotions of unfairly. I've distracted the world's attention from important issues of real people in real places. I've potentially compromised the safety of real people. I've helped lend credence to the lies of the regimes. I am sorry. I've hurt people with whom I share a side and a struggle. That matters. I've hurt causes I believe in sincerely. That is wrong. It started innocently enough without any intention whatsoever of creating a massive hoax or duping the world. Ever since I was a child I've wanted to write fiction, but when my first attempts met with universal rejection, I took a more serious look at my own work and realised that I couldn't write conversation in a natural way nor could I convincingly write characters who weren't me. I tried to get better and did various exercises. Eventually, I would set up a number of profiles on dating sites with identities that were not my own as ways of interacting with real people in conversation but with a different personality than my own.

Ever since my childhood I'd felt very connected to the cultures and peoples of the Middle East. It's something that I came by naturally. My mother had taught English in Turkey before I was born, and my father had been involved with Middle East refugee issues when they met. I'm also an argumentative sort and a bit of a nerd. I was involved with numerous online science-fiction/alternate-history discussion lists and, as a part of that process, I saw lots of incredibly ignorant and stupid positions repeated on the Middle East. I noticed that when I, a person with a distinctly English name, made comments on the Middle East, the facts I presented were ignored and I found myself accused of hating America, Jews, etc. I wondered idly whether the same ideas presented by someone with a distinctly Arab and female identity would have the same reaction.

So, I invented her. First, she was just a name – Amina Arraf. She commented on blogs and talkbacks on news sites. Eventually, I set up an email for her. She joined the same lists I was already on and posted responses in her name. And, almost immediately, friendly and solicitous comments appeared on mine. It was intriguing. That likely would have been the end of it. I'd just keep her as a nearly anonymous handle for commenting on issues that mattered to me but – Amina came alive. I could hear her voice, and that voice and personality were clear and strong. Amina was funny and smart, and equal parts infuriating and flirtatious. She struggled with her religious beliefs and sexuality, wondered about living in America as an Arab. She wanted to find a way to balance her religion and her sexuality, her desire to be both a patriotic American and a patriotic Arab. Amina was clever and fun, and had a story and voice and I started writing it, almost as though she were dictating to me. Some of her details were mine, some were those of a dozen other friends borrowed liberally, others were purely her from the get go.

And I did something really, really stupid at that point. I should have let the original brief experiment in nerd psychology go and, if I continued to hear the Amina voice, I should just use it in a novel.

I didn't. Instead, I enjoyed puppeting this woman who never was. I knew what she looked like in my head and I grabbed photos of a woman whom I have never met who looked exactly like what Amina should look like. That was stupid and possibly evil of me, and I'm really, really sorry about that. I gave Amina a Facebook page. She soon had friends and admirers. Amina kept growing. And I kept trying to kill her. Her story was great. I can easily write in Amina's voice because I know her like she was a real person. I know what she likes and what she dislikes. How she feels and what makes her angry or elates her.

It was a terrible time suck, but it was fun. And, regularly, I tried to stop. Amina moved overseas, she dropped out of sight repeatedly and so on and so forth. I meant to stop her, but it was hard. I'd read news stories and I'd find myself fighting the urge to respond as Amina and occasionally giving in.

I wasn't trying to pick fights or stir up controversy. I was instead trying to enlighten people. I posted comments on a blog. The owner asked me to contribute columns. I set up a blog to publish some of the things I'd written as Amina and, maybe, get a few comments. I didn't expect anyone to read it or to care if they did. In the first month and more it was up, it received only a few visits. That was more than I had expected.

Then, I wrote a perfect little story about the situation in Syria and the mutual affection between father and daughter – and to my shock, it went viral. Everything spiralled out of control. I couldn't think of how to shut Amina down – It just kept on growing –

And now, I have ended it. She is me. She never really existed. I feel like I'm in some ways the worst person in the world. I've hurt a lot of people, including people who thought of me, when I was her, as a good friend. I want to apologise clearly and explicitly and personally to Jelena Lecic, Paula Brooks, Sandra Bagaria and Scott Palter. Each of them, in very different ways, was hurt deeply by me and each of them will get a personal apology from me. Each of them is more than entitled to hit me.

I didn't mean to hurt them.

I didn't mean to harm anyone who is upset. I didn't mean to hurt the causes which I myself believe in. I didn't mean to malign anyone. My intentions were good. I got carried away. I owe apologies to those I hurt and will do all in my power to make things right. I only wanted to set forth real information through the use of artfully crafted fiction. I was too successful and I was too caught up in what I was doing. I ignored the consequences of my action.

I am sorry.

CHORUS enter.

I want to turn the focus away from me and urge everyone to concentrate on the real issues, the real heroes, the real people struggling to bring freedom to the Arab world. I have only distracted from real people and real problems. Those continue. Please focus on them.

TOM: Posted by …
At 14:28.

TOM and AMINA exit.

THE END OF THE BEGINNING

CHORUS 1: We represent adult and children's authors of all genres, including illustrators. If you would like to submit a manuscript or proposal, please send us a query letter, a synopsis of the work, a sample chapter and a brief resume.

CHORUS 3: Full Frame Pictures is interested in new writers and projects. We deal mostly with finished screenplays, but will occasionally get involved at an earlier, concept or treatment stage. Please send a logline and a short, one paragraph description, with a brief introduction. If we're interested in reading more, we'll email you a release form and will invite you to submit further material.

CHORUS 1: Sadly we are unable to offer a full script reading service and will only contact writers if we feel that their work fits into the artistic vision of the theatre and we are able to give them particular advice or help.

CHORUS 3: If an SAE is not enclosed the script will be recycled at the end of the process.

(Pause.)

CHORUS 1: Pitch it.

CHORUS 2: […]

CHORUS 1: Go on. Pitch it to me. I haven't got all day.

CHORUS 2: Okay. So, it's the story of a fat middle-aged American postgraduate student who takes on this fake online persona of a young pretty Syrian lesbian living through the uprisings. He – she has an online relationship with another man pretending to be a woman. *(Beat.)*

Amazing. She gets kidnapped. The story goes viral.
Online activists, human rights organisations, the frigging
State Department all get involved. He eventually gets
uncovered. And all hell breaks loose.

CHORUS 3: *(Beat.)* Okay – but haven't people had enough of
the Arab Spring? It's kind of old hat now.
It's all a bit too Kipling for my taste – your new-caught,
sullen peoples, half-devil and half-child.

(Pause.)

CHORUS 1: I think it's got legs actually. The fictitious tale of a
noble savage with a dark twist. It's taut. It's timely.
Get on the phone with the casting department. We'll need
someone with those untrustworthy sexy postcolonial looks.
Freida Pinto. You know – a modern-day Pocahontas.

CHORUS 3: I'm on it.

CHORUS 1: And writers. *(Beat.)* We'll need someone with real
flair.

The End.

SOUNDS OF THE MACHINE

These things can happen in any section.
They are nonetheless essential parts of the play.

The Wonder Woman theme song

The hook on Childish Gambino's 'Outside'

The refrain of 'Go Down Moses'

The first verse of 'Hush (Somebody' Calling My Name)'

John Legend's hook on Kanye West's 'Blame Game'

The hook on Tyga's 'Lap Dance'

The hook on Kanye West's 'Power'

WWW.OBERONBOOKS.COM

Follow us on www.twitter.com/@oberonbooks
& www.facebook.com/oberonbook